HOW TO HANDLE

BUSINESS CRISIS

Transforming Business Challenges into Success Stories.

LYNNE RUFFIN

Table of contents

Introduction   **5**

Understanding the Nature of Business Crise   5

Chapter One   **10**

Preparation Phase   10

Risk Assessment and Mitigation   10

Crisis Response Team Formation   13

Chapter Two   **20**

Early Warning Signs: Identifying Operational Red Flags and Preemptively Monitoring to Protect Company Health   20

Identifying Warning Signs in Business Operations   21

Proactive Monitoring Strategies   24

Chapter Three   **30**

Communication Strategies   30

Internal Communication Protocols   31

External Stakeholder Engagement   33

Case Studies: Crisis Management That Works 39

Chapter Four   **42**

Decision-Making Under Pressure   42

Swift and Effective Decision-Making Processes 42

Leadership Strategies for Crisis Management 45

Case Studies: Learning from Judging and Crisis Management   52

Chapter Five   **55**

Operational Continuity 55

Maintaining Essential Functions 55

Contingency Planning and Implementation 57

Chapter Six **62**

Learning from Crisis 62

Post-crisis Evaluation and Analysis 62

Modifying for Robustness in the Future 64

Chapter Seven **69**

Case Studies 69

Chapter Eight **76**

Legal and Ethical Considerations 76

Navigating Legal Challenges 76

Upholding Ethical Standards during Crisis 79

Chapter Nine **84**

Rebuilding and Recovery 84

Reestablishing Trust and Reputation 84

Strategies for Business Recovery 87

Conclusion **92**

Introduction

Understanding the Nature of Business Crise

In the ever-evolving world of business, crisis circumstances are unanticipated storms that have the ability to interrupt regular corporate operations. One of the things that makes these crises unique is their unpredictable nature, regardless of whether they include financial collapses, operational lapses, or reputational issues. Acknowledging the unpredictable nature of the circumstance is the first step towards building resilience.

Examining the internal and external elements that lead to business crises is essential to understanding their nature. Numerous things, such as bad decision-making, improper financial management, and outside pressures like recessions, might serve as triggers. Using this data forms the basis for implementing preventive measures and developing a structured preparation culture inside businesses.

Examining a crisis's internal organization exposes a number of traits and trends. These incidents are often followed by a feeling of urgency, heightened scrutiny, and an expeditious escalation of the issue. Organizations may effectively navigate through the crisis lifecycle and build situation-specific resolution options by looking at these components.

It is possible to learn important lessons from past company disasters. Case studies provide insights from both wins and losses, which aids companies in improving their crisis response plans. Decision-making and leadership become even more important in times of crisis, highlighting the importance of people in guiding businesses through difficult times.

In the digital world, crisis situations happen instantly on many channels, which increases their impact. Using effective communication strategies, managing the digital narrative, and acting quickly are all essential components of crisis management.

Stakeholders are impacted by business crises in addition to the company. Open communication and building trust with vendors, customers, staff, and the community at large are essential to the healing process.

Planning helps organizations navigate through disasters like a compass. When organizations have comprehensive risk assessments, mitigation strategies, crisis response teams, and scenario planning in place, they are better equipped to react quickly to issues.

Growth of an organization requires both post-crisis evaluation and ongoing development. Organizations may ensure that they evolve and adapt with every interaction by reevaluating crisis management techniques, focusing on specific approaches, and embracing a continuous improvement mindset.

In conclusion, building adaptable, resilient businesses starts with developing an understanding of the characteristics of business crises. Understanding the volatility of the terrain, researching crisis causes, learning from the past, and emphasizing the role of the human element in leadership are all necessary. In today's digital environment, stakeholder management and effective communication are essential. Developing resilience in the face of uncertainty requires planning, reflecting after a catastrophe, and evolving over time.

Chapter One

Preparation Phase

The capacity to anticipate and surmount unanticipated obstacles is essential in the dynamic corporate world. The preparation phase, which is the cornerstone for businesses looking to build resilience, is built on the creation of a crisis response team as well as risk assessment and mitigation. This comprehensive strategy provides firms with the tools they need to not only foresee potential threats but also to act swiftly and forcefully when a calamity strikes.

Risk Assessment and Mitigation

Risk assessment is the proactive process of identifying, looking into, and evaluating any hazards that could have an impact on a business. These risks might come from a number of places, including unforeseen circumstances, changes in the law, the dynamics of the external market, or internal business processes. The goal of risk assessment is to comprehend the possibility and probable effect of various risks, which aids businesses in creating mitigation strategies.

Identification of Potential Risks

The first phase of risk assessment is a thorough examination of every aspect of the company. This covers a wide variety of subjects, including financial operations, human resources, supply chain management, and regulatory compliance. Organizations that carefully examine each area may find weak points and potential causes of disturbance.

Analyzing Effect and Probability

Because risks are not all created equal, prioritizing requires an understanding of each risk's possibility and effect. Firms may optimize their resource use by using risk probability and consequence classification. This phase requires careful balance in order to handle both high-impact, low-likelihood occurrences and more likely hazards.

Developing Mitigation Strategies

After hazards are identified and examined, the next stage is to develop mitigation alternatives. The goal of these strategies is to lessen the likelihood or impact of known threats. These might include expanding your supply base, putting in place strict internal controls, getting insurance, or creating backup plans. These tactics will only be effective if they align with the particular risks identified during the evaluation.

Continuous Monitoring and Adjustment

Risk assessment is not a one-time event, but rather an ongoing activity. Markets shift, regulations change, and new risks arise. To guarantee that their risk reduction tactics remain suitable and effective, businesses must establish procedures for continuous evaluation and modification.

Crisis Response Team Formation

A readiness plan is strategically implemented via the formation of a crisis response team, even if risk assessment and mitigation provide the framework for resilience. This crew is on the front lines during disasters, leading a coordinated response to lessen the effects and speed up recovery.

Selecting Vital Team Members

Choosing essential team members is the first stage in creating a strong crisis response team. These people must possess a wide range of skills, viewpoints, and experiences. Ideally, the team should include representatives from many departments, including as senior leadership, operations, finance, legal, and communications.

Define Positions and Responsibilities

Clarity is essential in times of distress. Each team member's roles and duties must be clearly stated in order to ensure that there are no misunderstandings throughout the response. To do this, it must be decided who will be in charge of coordinating with other parties, communicating, allocating resources, and making decisions.

Establishing Communication Protocols

Effective communication is critical to a crisis's success. By defining explicit communication protocols, the crisis response team can ensure smooth information flow. This includes creating a unified platform for information exchange, establishing reporting guidelines, and scheduling frequent briefings.

Putting Training and Simulations into Practice

Training drills and role-playing improve readiness. Crisis response teams should often practice simulated scenarios so they can mimic real-world circumstances. These drills hone the team's reaction skills and suggest areas where the crisis management strategy should be improved.

Integrating Outside Resources

Since crises seldom occur in a vacuum, it is essential to include outside resources into the crisis response strategy. It could be crucial for this to coordinate with outside advisors, legal specialists, public relations specialists, or industry experts. Establishing these connections in advance guarantees a thorough and timely reaction in case of an emergency.

Maintaining Mental Hardiness

Human factor is more important in crisis response than technological factor. Team members must be ready to withstand the strain and anxiety that accompany emergencies. Training programs should include stress management, resilience development, and a cooperative team culture.

Using Risk Mitigation, Assessment, and Crisis Response Together

The true power of the preparation stage lies in the way risk assessment, mitigation, and crisis response team creation interact. Risk assessment identifies potential risks, mitigation strategies strengthen the organization's defenses against them, and the crisis response team is prepared to respond quickly and effectively to obstacles.

A Harmonious Framework for Adaptability

Together, these elements provide a cohesive resilience structure. The company does more than just prepare for disasters; it actively guards against unforeseen setbacks. Proactive action not only lessens the effects of crises but also improves the organization's ability to recover from them.

Flexibility and Quickness

Planning is when an organization gains its agility and flexibility. Businesses adapt to the ever-changing business environment by improving their crisis response plan, regularly evaluating risks, and adjusting mitigation strategies. This adaptability gives businesses a competitive edge by allowing them to quickly overcome unforeseen obstacles.

Building Trust Among Stakeholders

Stakeholders who reward firms that demonstrate resilience and preparation include customers, employees, investors, and partners. The organization's systematic approach to risk assessment, mitigation, and crisis response team development sends a strong message to stakeholders: it is proactive, strategic, and committed to maintaining business continuity.

Forming the Foundation for Business Continuity

To sum up, the planning process, which encompasses risk assessment, mitigation, and the establishment of a crisis response team, builds a robust foundation for business continuity. It is a strategic attitude that infuses the company culture rather than just a to-do list. After overcoming the turbulent business environment, companies become stronger and more resilient by investing in an all-encompassing strategy. They can also withstand disasters better.

Chapter Two

Early Warning Signs: Identifying Operational Red Flags and Preemptively Monitoring to Protect Company Health

In the complex world of business, being able to recognize early warning signs is similar to having a radar system that can predict storms before they materialize. This proactive approach entails using proactive monitoring strategies in addition to identifying warning signs in business operations. Companies that master this skill not only protect themselves from disasters but also position themselves to confront issues head-on and emerge stronger on the other side.

Identifying Warning Signs in Business Operations

Financial Distress Indicators

The first item to closely examine for warning signs is the organization's financial situation. A decline in profitability, an increase in debt, irregular cash flow, or late payments are all indicators of possible financial trouble. Regular audits, financial statement reviews, and regular monitoring of important financial data are all considered essential activities.

Operational Inefficiencies

Operational red flags usually manifest as inefficiencies that impede efficiency and production. Rising error rates, rising production costs, and project schedule delays might all be signs of deeper operational problems. Process audits, regular performance reviews, and employee feedback systems may all be used to quickly identify and address these inefficiencies.

Declining Customer Satisfaction Level

Since every business depends on its customers, a decline in customer satisfaction should be taken seriously. A noticeable decline in recurring business, an increase in customer complaints, or unfavorable reviews might all be signs of problems with the quality of the product, the level of customer service, or general contentment. Surveys of customer satisfaction and the regular introduction of consumer feedback systems may provide valuable insights.

Employee Disengagement

Employee dissatisfaction may raise internal issues. High turnover rates, low employee morale, and increased absenteeism may all be signs of more serious problems. Frequent employee surveys, open lines of communication inside the company, and one-on-one meetings are all useful tools for tracking and improving employee engagement.

Regulatory Compliance Problems

Changes in the regulatory environment or breaking current rules may be associated with serious risks. Red signals include things like increased regulatory agency scrutiny, legal problems, or punishments. Regular legal compliance audits and keeping up with industry standards are essential for identifying and resolving any compliance issues.

Shifts in the Market and Competition Pressure

Shifts in client preferences or increased competition might be warning signs in the dynamic business environment. A sharp decline in sales, a shift in the competitive landscape, or a rapid loss of market share might all point to the need for strategic changes. Continuous observation of market research, competitive analysis, and industry developments is necessary for early identification.

Proactive Monitoring Strategies

Real-Time Financial Monitoring

By using real-time financial monitoring systems, organizations may measure important financial metrics on a regular basis. Automatic technology may send out alarms when certain standards are broken, allowing for quick answers to financial worries. This real-time visibility is essential for identifying such problems early and taking appropriate action before they worsen.

Tracking KPIs (Key Performance Indicators)

By developing a strong set of KPIs and regularly reviewing them, it is possible to get a complete picture of the performance of the business. Measuring critical performance indicators including employee engagement, customer happiness, and operational efficiency is necessary to achieve this. It is advised to take proactive measures as early warning signs when projected KPIs diverge.

Data analytics and predictive modeling

Using predictive modeling and data analytics, organizations may find patterns and trends that would not be apparent with routine monitoring. Predictive models may help businesses take preventative measures by analyzing current data and looking for patterns that may indicate future problems.

Customer feedback and sentiment analysis

It is essential to have procedures for quickly gathering and evaluating consumer input. Online surveys, attitude analysis software, and social media observation may reveal fresh problems and provide information on how satisfied customers are. Resolving client issues proactively may lessen the risk of reputational damage.

Staff surveys and feedback loops

Regular staff surveys and feedback loops provide an ongoing means of monitoring the internal pulse of the company. Recognizing patterns in employee satisfaction, handling grievances, and encouraging open communication all contribute to the early identification of issues relating to employees and a good corporate culture.

Continued Market Analysis

To stay ahead of changes in the market and pressure from competitors, ongoing market research is necessary. It is recommended that companies allocate resources to the following: regular market evaluations, competitor method research, and industry trend tracking. By using this proactive approach, firms may quickly adapt to changing market conditions.

Risk evaluations and preparation for scenarios

Through comprehensive risk assessments and scenario planning, firms may detect unforeseen obstacles. By closely studying diverse occurrences and the associated risks, businesses may develop backup plans and reaction strategies. This proactive planning reduces the impact of unforeseen events.

The Merger of Identification and Proactive Monitoring

Red flag detection and proactive monitoring together are a powerful tool for protecting your company's wellbeing. The use of proactive monitoring techniques is predicated on the early identification of warning signs, which offers a constant feedback loop that fosters organizational adaptability and resilience.

Promoting an Alert Culture

When proactive monitoring and red flag identification are ingrained in the corporate culture, an awareness culture is created. When every team member is empowered to raise concerns and is aware of potential problems, the company responds more quickly.

Enhancing Decision-Making

The knowledge obtained from proactive monitoring and early warning indicators greatly improves decision-making. Executives may steer their company away from potential issues and toward strategic possibilities by using real-time data and predictive analytics to make prompt, well-informed choices.

Mitigating the Impact of Emergencies

Proactive monitoring and early identification most likely have the greatest impact on lessening the aftermath of catastrophes. By addressing problems early on and protecting their assets, good name, and regular business operations, organizations may prevent crises from becoming worse.

Chapter Three

Communication Strategies

Good communication is essential in the unstable atmosphere of a corporate crisis since it may either make things worse or pave the way for recovery. This calls for a two-pronged strategy that combines ways of external stakeholder engagement for open and comforting interactions with internal communication standards for cohesive team management. When an organization uses these communication strategies well, it may weather crises and come out stronger and with its reputation intact.

Internal Communication Protocols

Sincere and Open Leadership Discussion

In times of crisis, leaders play a critical role in assisting the company in managing uncertainty. It is imperative that the leadership openly communicates, presents the facts of the problem, and outlines the actions being taken. The internal team therefore becomes more reliable and cohesive.

Explicit Roles and Responsibilities

Uncertainty in one's employment might lead to confusion and inefficiency during a crisis. Clearly defining the duties and responsibilities of each team member helps to produce a coordinated response. To do this, decision-makers, communication hubs, and staff members responsible for executing certain crisis management tasks must be identified.

Data Exchange and Instantaneous Updates

Being quick with communications during a crisis is essential. Establishing real-time communication channels, such instant messaging software or specialized crisis communication tools, makes it possible to share information quickly. This guarantees the coordinated and knowledgeable reaction efforts of the internal team.

Employee Support Mechanisms

Crises might negatively impact the wellbeing of employees. A company demonstrates its concern for the welfare of its employees by implementing support systems such as frequent check-ins, counseling services, and open platforms for grievances. During hard circumstances, this proactive strategy helps sustain productivity and morale.

Guidelines and Models

It's critical to conduct frequent training and simulations to prepare the internal team for crisis situations. By performing simulated crisis situations, staff members may hone their responsibilities and reactions, enabling a better coordinated and successful response in the event of a real crisis. Through training, staff members also get acquainted with the organization's crisis communication procedures.

External Stakeholder Engagement

Clear and Timely External Communication

Equally important is timely and open contact with the outside world. Establishing proactive communication, identifying difficulties, and presenting a clear plan of action for overcoming them establish confidence with external stakeholders. Since mistrust may arise from silence or delayed information, transparency is essential to crisis communication.

Customized Letters to Different Parties

Many stakeholders may have varying expectations and concerns during a crisis. Messages that are tailored to the specific requirements of suppliers, investors, consumers, and the larger community are more relevant and effective. Understanding the diverse viewpoints held by each stakeholder group is essential to productive participation.

Management of Social Media

In the digital era, social media is a fantastic information amplifier. Companies must aggressively monitor their social media accounts during a crisis, answering inquiries, providing updates, and dispelling misinformation. Social media platforms may be used not just for communication but also for research on public attitude.

Collaboration Partnerships

Building cooperative relationships with other groups—such as advocacy groups, trade associations, or governmental organizations—may improve crisis communication operations. These collaborations help to create a coordinated response by bringing in resources and assistance that may be crucial to finding a solution.

Always Creating New Connections

Successful crisis communication requires ongoing connection development; reactive crisis communication is insufficient. Companies that take the time to build long-lasting relationships with external stakeholders outside of crisis situations often find that these stakeholders are more empathetic and forgiving during times of adversity.

Media Relations and Spokesperson Training

The media has a crucial role in influencing public perception during a crisis. Businesses should spend money on media relations strategies and spokesperson training if they want to guarantee that their message is understood correctly and in line with their core beliefs. A recognized spokesperson may provide a coherent and well-controlled story.

The Interaction of Internal and External Communication

Success in crisis communication depends on the smooth operation of internal and external communication systems. A breakdown in internal communication might result in inconsistent outward messaging that could jeopardize trust. On the other hand, opinions from outside stakeholders may have an impact on internal morale. It is essential that these two elements work together.

Alignment of Messages

Maintaining consistency between internal and external communications is essential for maintaining credibility. Internal teams should be aware of external messaging and vice versa to prevent inconsistencies. Building trust with audiences, both internal and external, is facilitated by consistent messaging.

Employee Assistance in Outward Communications

During emergency situations, employees might act as strong advocates. Workers who get clear internal communications from their companies act as brand ambassadors, communicating a unified message to stakeholders outside the company. Investing in internal communication helps with external reputation management.

Gentle Adjustments

It could be necessary to modify communication strategies in a dynamic crisis scenario. Feedback loops between the teams in charge of internal and external communication may be used to provide responses. Being adaptable is essential for responding to changing circumstances and stakeholder viewpoints.

Learning From the Past

Businesses should use the lessons learned from past crises to improve their communication strategies. It is informative to look at the successes and shortcomings of both internal and external communication. This strategy of recurrent learning improves crisis communication protocols.

Case Studies: Crisis Management That Works

Examining case studies of businesses that effectively handled crises via effective communication strategies demonstrates how these concepts are really put into practice.

Johnson & Johnson's Tylenol Crisis

When seven people died in 1982 after ingesting tainted Tylenol pills, Johnson & Johnson had a problem. Public safety was suggested by the company's open lines of contact, prompt recall, and coordination with law enforcement. In addition to maintaining their reputation, Johnson & Johnson set a standard for crisis management by using a crisis communication plan.

Southwest Airlines' Emergency Landing

2018 saw the death of a passenger aboard a Southwest Airlines aircraft after an emergency landing. The airline demonstrated its concern for passenger safety by getting in touch with internal and external stakeholders promptly and tactfully. Sincere apologies, forthright updates, and proactive measures all contributed to the restoration of confidence.

To put it simply, understanding internal communication procedures as well as external stakeholder engagement is essential to the art of crisis communication. Companies that prioritize open and honest communication, invest in the health and welfare of their employees, and tailor messaging to individual stakeholders are better equipped to handle crisis circumstances. When internal and external communication collaborate to guarantee a coordinated response and build trust, a crisis may ultimately be turned into a chance for organizational development and resilience.

Chapter Four

Decision-Making Under Pressure

In times of high risks and uncertainty, an organization's capacity to withstand a business crisis depends on its ability to make decisions. Navigating the intricacies of quick decision-making procedures in conjunction with strategic leadership is essential for surviving a crisis and emerging from it stronger.

Swift and Effective Decision-Making Processes

Clear Structures for Making Decisions

Having clear frameworks for decision-making is essential to managing emergencies. When things are quiet, organizations should establish roles, responsibilities, and decision-making procedures. In times of crisis, this clarity ensures that decisions be made quickly, reducing uncertainty and delays.

Modifiable Structures for Decision-Making

In an emergency, quick decision-making is essential. In environments that are changing quickly, hierarchical systems may become problematic. Agile decision-making techniques, including cross-functional crisis response teams, facilitate prompt evaluations, cooperative problem-solving, and prompt decision-implementation. This adaptability is required to deal with the changing circumstances of a crisis.

Decision-Making Based on Information

In the era of information, data becomes an extremely powerful tool for decision-making. Businesses should place a strong emphasis on the collection, processing, and analysis of data in real time. Data-driven decision-making provides executives with insights into how a situation is changing so they may make decisions based on accurate and current information.

Creating Backup Plans and Scenarios

Making proactive decisions means planning ahead and creating backup plans by imagining possible scenarios. situation planning is developing reaction strategies for every possible crisis situation. By ensuring that decision-makers have a range of options at their disposal, this preparedness shortens the time needed for them to respond in an emergency.

Fast Channels of Contact

Making decisions quickly requires quick communication lines. When effective lines of communication are established, such instant messaging software or dedicated crisis communication platforms, information may be shared more quickly. In an emergency, decision-makers must coordinate and move quickly, which requires prompt communication.

Leadership Strategies for Crisis Management

Conclusive Advice

Decisiveness is a hallmark of effective crisis leadership. Leaders have to act quickly to make difficult choices even in the face of uncertainty. The capacity to assess risks, weigh options, and make choices quickly instills more trust in the team and stakeholders. Determinate leadership builds an organizational response that is robust and proactive.

Communication that is Open and Transparent

An essential element of effective crisis leadership is transparent and sincere communication. It is imperative that executives communicate clearly about the severity of the issue, potential obstacles, and the organization's crisis management plan. Trust between internal teams and external stakeholders is fostered via transparency, which creates a common understanding of the future course.

Kindness and Collective Support

Empathy in leadership is essential during crisis times. Supervisors need to be aware of the emotional toll employees bear while working. Fostering a culture of compassion, offering choices for help, and demonstrating empathy all contribute to maintaining team morale and cohesiveness. In hard times, a culture that is supportive fosters resilience and loyalty.

Gentle Leadership Methods

Different situations call for different approaches to leadership. Understanding the unique components of a crisis and modifying one's leadership style accordingly are key components of adaptive leadership. Whether it's a reputational crisis requiring great communication skills or a financial catastrophe requiring strategic financial expertise, leaders must adapt their strategies to suit each unique set of circumstances.

Owning Up to Errors

Crises most likely don't always have a great conclusion. Effective leaders create an environment where mistakes are shared and learned from. Executives were required to do thorough post-crisis appraisals, examine decision-making procedures, and identify areas that needed improvement once the crisis ended. This methodical approach aids in the ongoing improvement of crisis response strategies and education.

Creating a Collaborative Culture

Collaborating is essential for effectively managing emergencies. Leaders should promote a collaborative atmosphere where different viewpoints are valued and teams function well. Building a sense of trust and camaraderie among team members improves the group's ability to make decisions and handle problems, which increases the firm's resilience.

Long-Term Objectives Despite Immediate Stress

Leading amid a crisis requires a deft balancing act between immediate demands and long-term goals. While urgent problems need quick fixes, CEOs also need to focus on the long-term objectives of the company. Aligning immediate crisis management with long-term development and sustainability goals is a key element of strategic decision-making.

The Connection Between Fast Decision-Making and Excellent Leadership

The key to effective crisis management is the intersection of strong leadership and quick decision-making procedures. Decision-making is affected by leadership, and rapid choices improve the credibility of the leader. Navigating a company through the complexities of a crisis requires this kind of mutually beneficial teamwork.

Alignment of Decision-Making and Leadership Vision

Effective leaders act in accordance with their vision when faced with a crisis. This alignment ensures a planned and coordinated approach to crisis management. When the leadership vision and decision-making process align, an organization has the ability to overcome challenges and emerges with a clear path forward.

Motivating Colleagues to Take Initiative

Encouraging decision-makers inside the company to have the authority they merit at all levels is necessary for effective leadership. During a crisis, leaders should assign tasks and provide teams the freedom to choose within their areas of expertise. This speeds up the decision-making process and taps into the collective intelligence of the business.

Trust is the Basis

Trust is a need for both quick decision-making and effective leadership. Leaders build a culture of trust with internal and external stakeholders, facilitating quick decision-making. When a team is trusted to make decisions, they feel more confident in doing so because they know their leaders value and will stand by them.

Outlining the Justification for the Choice

Explaining the reasoning behind choices is a sign of excellent leadership. Leaders should provide a clear and concise justification for every action they make. When there is open and honest communication among team members, the group is better able to understand the strategic direction and come together around shared objectives.

Adaptable Management in a Changing Setting

Adaptive leadership is essential in a dynamic crisis situation. When a crisis develops, leaders must be flexible and adjust their plans and tactics accordingly. This adaptability guarantees that the leadership of the company will continue to be successful even in the face of unanticipated obstacles and uncertainty.

Case Studies: Learning from Judging and Crisis Management

Examining case studies of businesses that demonstrated crisis management and sound decision-making provides important context for understanding how to implement these ideas.

NASA's Apollo 13 Mission

During NASA's Apollo 13 mission, an oxygen tank explosion created a potentially disastrous situation. Flight Director Gene Kranz is an example of how leadership demonstrated decisive decision-making under extreme pressure. Collaboratively, they overcame obstacles, adjusted to changing conditions, and returned the astronauts to Earth without incident. The experience stressed the need of adaptable leadership and quick decision-making in the face of unanticipated obstacles.

IBM's Response to the Issue with Year 2000

As 2000 approached, worries about the potential effects of the Y2K bug on computer systems increased. With Lou Gerstner leading IBM, the company demonstrated bold decision-making by aggressively addressing the Y2K crisis. IBM's prompt action and open channels of contact with customers during the Y2K changeover eased concerns and established the company as a leader in crisis management.

Managing a corporate crisis requires orchestration, which is a symphony of quick decisions and strong leadership abilities. Proven leaders set the example for excellent decision-making by fostering an environment of openness, confidence, and adaptability. The interaction between leadership vision and decision logic creates a perfect link.

Chapter Five

Operational Continuity

Businesses must give up everything else to prioritize the upkeep of their operations during times of crisis. When things go rough, the capacity to carry on with crucial operations becomes essential for survival and lessens the effects of setbacks. The execution of backup plans must be properly combined with the upkeep of essential services in order to carry out this crucial duty.

Maintaining Essential Functions

The first step in guaranteeing operational continuity is to identify the critical functions. Businesses have a need to be very transparent about the tasks that are most important to them. These are the operations that might possibly cause the company serious harm if they are interrupted. Examples include handling supply chain management, handling financial transactions, and offering customer assistance.

After these crucial duties are identified, the emphasis switches to creating backup and redundancy plans for those responsibilities. You will need to expand the number of providers you have accessible, build alternate communication routes, and invest in reliable technology in order to do this. The goal is to establish a solid foundation that will allow the main business to continue operating while withstanding unforeseen shocks.

It is essential to regularly assess risks and vulnerabilities. Through the implementation of comprehensive risk assessments, companies may anticipate potential issues and proactively address them. Building connections with other suppliers, for instance, might reduce the chance of supply chain interruptions in the event that a company becomes too dependent on one particular source.

Contingency Planning and Implementation

Contingency planning is the proactive approach to crisis management. It necessitates developing comprehensive plans and procedures so that, in the event of unforeseen circumstances, prompt action may be taken. A variety of scenarios are covered by this readiness, such as global pandemics, cyberattacks, and natural disasters.

- ❖ **Risk Assessment:** Businesses must conduct a thorough risk assessment in order to detect potential crises that might affect their operations. This necessitates understanding the likelihood and potential consequences of each risk.

- ❖ **Analysis of Business Impact:** Analyzing the potential effects of any interruptions on important operations is essential. This stage helps to prioritize tasks that must be completed as soon as possible during a crisis, using the resources available.

- ❖ **Communication Protocols:** To effectively handle a crisis, open lines of communication must be established. It is necessary to establish roles and responsibilities, communication channels, and real-time updating systems.

- ❖ **Training and exercises:** Employees should become proficient in the contingency plan via recurring training sessions and exercises. This ensures a coordinated reaction in the event of a disaster, minimizing the margin for mistake in high-stakes situations.

- ❖ **Technology Infrastructure:** Building a robust technology infrastructure is an essential part of being ready for emergencies. This includes backup systems, safe data storage, and cloud-based solutions that enable remote work when necessary.

- ❖ **Partnership with Interest Parties:** Maintaining communication with stakeholders, including as suppliers, customers, and regulatory agencies, is essential. Collaborating ensures a well-organized endeavor to address obstacles together and maintain business continuity.

Just as important as the creation of backup plans is how they are carried out. In times of crisis, businesses must respond quickly to implement these strategies. All organizational levels must work together, communicate effectively, and make decisions quickly.

A fundamental feature of the dynamic corporate environment is crises. Operational continuity is not just a problem-solving tactic; it is a strategic objective that businesses must instill in their corporate DNA. Organizations may demonstrate resilience and flexibility in unpredictable times by implementing efficient contingency plans and carrying on with critical activities.

Organizations are better positioned to not just survive but also thrive in the midst of disaster by taking a proactive approach to finding weaknesses, making technological investments, and cultivating a culture of readiness. Long-term success will depend on operational stability even as the business environment changes.

Chapter Six

Learning from Crisis

Learning from a crisis after it has occurred is not only essential, but it is also strategically necessary for companies that want to thrive in an unstable environment. The strategy includes a thorough post-crisis assessment and analysis, which is followed by the implementation of enhancements that boost resilience going forward.

Post-crisis Evaluation and Analysis

Evaluation of Reaction Effectiveness: After a crisis, businesses need to assess how well their reaction procedures are working. This include assessing how well lines of communication performed, how well everyone coordinated throughout the crisis, and how well backup plans were put into place.

The method of identifying defects: Finding gaps in current systems is a critical part of learning from a catastrophe. This include pinpointing the response's weak points, vulnerabilities that were made public, and any holes in the backup plans that still need filling.

Stakeholder Feedback: Important information is generated when partners, clients, and employees provide input. Their feedback may draw attention to aspects of the crisis management strategy that an internal evaluation may have missed.

Timeline Analysis: Understanding the sequence of events and their effects is aided by examining the chronology of the crisis's occurrences. This inquiry may reveal significant circumstances and choices that affected the outcome.

Evaluation of Cost-Benefit: Analyzing the crisis response financially is essential. This necessitates weighing the advantages of the adopted remedies against the costs incurred during the crisis, both direct and indirect. It establishes a foundation for further investments in resilience measures.

Modifying for Robustness in the Future

- **Adaptation of Contingency Plans:** In light of the lessons learned, businesses should enhance and modify their contingency plans. This may include using fresh methods, adopting new technology, or adjusting the risk assessment to incorporate the knowledge gained from the most recent event.

- **Enhanced Methods of Communication:** Generally speaking, improving communication tactics is the first priority after a crisis. This entails improving internal communication channels, establishing more precise external communication standards, and making sure that stakeholders get timely and correct information.

- **Technology Investment:** Future-proofing a corporation requires a sound technological backbone. By making investments in cutting-edge technology, cybersecurity, and data protection, a business may stay ahead of the curve in terms of innovation and be safeguarded from potential disasters.

- **Crisis Simulation Exercises:** By conducting regular simulation exercises, organizations may assess the effectiveness of their backup plans. These exercises, which provide a realistic setting for practicing crisis responses and stressing areas that demand improvement, are participated in by employees of all levels.

- **Cultural Transition towards Adaptability:** Creating a mindset that views setbacks as opportunities for growth is essential to creating a resilient culture. This cultural transformation encourages adaptability, creativity, and a proactive approach to risk assessment and reduction.

- **Supply Chain Diversification:** Diversifying their supply chain becomes a strategic decision for companies that depend heavily on a small number of suppliers. This gives a more strong and robust supply network and lessens the effect of outages in a single source.

- **Regulatory Compliance Assessment:** It is essential to regularly evaluate and ensure compliance with relevant rules. Regulation changes or noncompliance may pose serious risks during a crisis, therefore businesses need to be informed of and abide by the law.

Learning from a disaster is a continuous process that goes beyond a quick recovery. It's a commitment to resiliency, flexibility, and ongoing development.

Post-crisis review provides a method for figuring out what worked, what didn't, and what may be improved.

Implementing changes involves more than just fixing the flaws that a crisis exposes; it also entails preparing for potential future problems. Businesses that actively learn from disasters, adapt, and preserve a strong corporate culture are not just survivors; they are positioned for long-term success in a market that is always evolving. As they say, "What doesn't kill you makes you stronger," and in the business sector, the ability to bounce back and develop from setbacks might be a key factor in success in the road.

Chapter Seven

Case Studies

Analyzing genuine case studies of successful crisis management offers crucial insights into the approaches and judgments that organizations apply when encountering hard situations. Here are a few notable examples:

Tylenol Poisoning Crisis of 1982

When seven individuals died after ingesting Tylenol capsules laced with cyanide in 1982, Johnson & Johnson was forced to face with a catastrophe. The company's reaction established a standard for handling crises. Instead of downplaying the circumstances, Johnson & Johnson took swift action. The recall of 31 million Tylenol bottles cost more than $100 million in losses. This proactive measure emphasized public safety and demonstrated corporate responsibility.

Key Takeaway: Transparency and prompt, decisive action may help minimize harm to the reputation and public confidence.

Toyota Recall Crisis (2009–2010)

Toyota, a company known for its commitment to quality, faced a serious problem when reports of unexpected acceleration in their cars began to surface. The company had to recall millions of cars, which damaged its brand and lost them a lot of money. Toyota acknowledged the issue, conducted thorough investigations, and implemented remedial actions as part of their response. They also improved communication with authorities and clients.

Key Point to Keep in Mind: Being honest in communication, taking responsibility for mistakes, and reacting appropriately are all part of reestablishing confidence.

Deepwater Horizon BP Oil Spill (2010)

The Deepwater Horizon oil leak is among the worst environmental catastrophes in recorded history. BP was scrutinized heavily because to its role in the catastrophe. In response, the corporation has pledged to manage the leak by devoting significant resources to it, establishing a $20 billion compensation fund, and interacting with federal authorities. Despite the accident's severity, BP's commitment to solving the problem and using the lessons it learned from it made rehabilitation easier.

Key Takeaway: Acknowledging responsibilities, cooperating with stakeholders, and making investments in solutions may all support healing.

The Discrimination Crisis at Airbnb in 2016

Airbnb was forced into a crisis when allegations of racism surfaced on its website. Users reported incidences of racism and racial profiling. Airbnb responded by implementing many measures, including the development of an anti-discrimination policy, the need for host education, and the formation of a staff to handle complaints pertaining to discrimination. These initiatives aimed to improve the platform's usability and inclusivity.

Key Takeaway: In order to address social issues, proactive legislation and ongoing efforts to promote diversity are essential.

The COVID-19 response from Zoom Video Communications (2020)

Due to the unanticipated increase in distant work during the COVID-19 pandemic, Zoom became a vital virtual communication tool. However, it was criticized for privacy and security flaws, which are sometimes referred to as "Zoombombing." Zoom responded quickly to address the issue by providing additional security measures, increasing transparency, and aggressively informing users of privacy protections.

Main Point to Remember: By placing a strong emphasis on user security and responding quickly to new threats, trust is created and preserved.

The Boeing 737 Max Crisis of 2019

Boeing found itself in a risky situation after two horrific incidents involving its 737 Max aircraft, which resulted in a global grounding. The disclosure of government oversights and design flaws made the issue worse. In response, Boeing halted production, assisted with inquiries, and made enhancements to address safety issues. The organization has promised to encourage openness and communication.

Key Point to Keep in Mind: Maintaining transparency, coordinating with authorities, and prioritizing safety are critical in the aviation industry.

The evaluations of these case studies highlight a number of characteristics of effective crisis management, such as emphasizing stakeholder trust, taking responsibility, acting quickly, and being truthful. These events highlight the need of learning from and responding to catastrophes effectively in order to not just weather the storm but to come out stronger on the other side. These real-world lessons serve as compass points for businesses hoping to develop and not just survive in the face of hardship in an ever-evolving business environment.

Chapter Eight

Legal and Ethical Considerations

Maintaining ethical standards and negotiating legal obstacles are essential elements of crisis management in the corporate world. Legal and ethical issues are critical in deciding how to proceed toward recovery and preserving stakeholder confidence when businesses face uncertainty.

Navigating Legal Challenges

Regulatory Adherence and Compliance: It is crucial to make sure that all relevant rules and regulations are followed. Legal difficulties may emerge during a crisis as a result of problems with personnel management, contractual duties, or data breaches. Companies need to be aware of the latest legal standards and act quickly to resolve any possible infractions.

Contrary to Expectations and Unforeseeability: Crises have the ability to interrupt contractual responsibilities and give rise to legal conflicts. It is essential to comprehend force majeure terms and when they apply. Mitigating legal disputes may be achieved by pursuing peaceful solutions and communicating openly about difficulties with parties.

Workforce Management and Employment Law: Legal concerns pertaining to the workforce often surface during times of crisis, particularly when choices are being made about furloughs, layoffs, or regulations governing remote work. Respecting employee well-being, communicating clearly, and abiding by employment rules are all necessary to stay out of legal hot water.

Privacy and Data Protection: As companies increasingly depend on digital channels, data security emerges as a crucial legal factor. During a crisis, data breaches may result in legal ramifications. It is critical to have strong cybersecurity safeguards in place, respond quickly to breaches, and abide by privacy regulations.

Accounting Openness and Disclosure: Financial openness is required by law in addition to being a moral precept. Precise and prompt financial reporting is essential, particularly in times of crisis. Deceiving stakeholders may result in legal ramifications and harm the standing of the organization.

Insurance Coverage and Claims: It's critical to comprehend the extent of insurance coverage and to file claims as soon as possible. If there is uncertainty or disagreement concerning coverage, legal challenges may occur. Companies and insurers should work together to successfully negotiate these obstacles.

Upholding Ethical Standards during Crisis

- **Reliability and Openness:** The first steps in upholding ethical standards are being sincere and open. Building confidence with stakeholders during a crisis requires honest communication about the difficulties encountered. False information has the potential to cause serious ethical transgressions as well as long-term reputational harm.

- **Stakeholder Consideration:** When making ethical decisions, it is important to take all stakeholders' interests into account. It is essential to strike a balance between the interests of investors, consumers, staff, and the larger community. Ethical resilience is enhanced by placing a higher value on long-term connections than on temporary advantages.

- **Corporate Social Responsibility (CSR):** One way to show off corporate social responsibility is via crisis management. During times of crisis, ethical organizations actively support the welfare of the community, demonstrating a commitment that goes beyond financial gain. This is in line with moral values and improves the reputation of the brand.

- **Employee Welfare and Fair Treatment:** How businesses handle their staff in times of crises is also a matter of ethics. Putting employee wellness first, treating people fairly, and maintaining open lines of communication all help to project an ethical image. Practices that are unethical, including discrimination or exploitation, may have long-term effects.

- **Environmental Responsibility:** Minimizing damage and upholding sustainable practices are ethical issues for enterprises that have an influence on the environment. Resolving conflicts while upholding environmental responsibility helps to create a more positive ethical narrative.

- **Community Engagement and Support:** Part of acting ethically is being involved in and giving back to the community. Businesses that provide resources, knowledge, or support during emergencies display ethical leadership and develop better links with the communities they serve.

Organizations may strengthen their image and develop resilience by managing legal issues and maintaining moral principles in times of crisis. Sustainable crisis management is based on the interaction of ethical concerns with legal compliance. Companies that put an emphasis on openness, justice, and a dedication to the welfare of society not only survive the storm better, but they also get more credibility and confidence from stakeholders. A strong foundation of legal and ethical principles acts as a compass in the complicated world of crises, pointing companies in the direction of ethical and sustainable actions.

Chapter Nine

Rebuilding and Recovery

After a catastrophe in the firm, there is a critical phase of reconstruction and recuperation that needs careful planning and a commitment to regaining confidence and reputation. Two essential elements of this approach are the implementation of efficient company recovery processes and the rebuilding of trust and reputation.

Reestablishing Trust and Reputation

Transparent Communication: Rebuilding trust begins with open communication. Acknowledge the issues that arose during the crisis, share the information that was gathered, and specify the steps being taken to make sure it doesn't happen again. Openness fosters trust and demonstrates a commitment to responsibility.

Acting as the Head: Honest leadership goes a long way toward facilitating trust rebuilding. Leaders that take responsibility for their actions, own up to their mistakes, and show a genuine desire for improvement inspire confidence. Sincerity engages stakeholders and repairs a tarnished image.

Stakeholder Engagement: Building relationships with stakeholders is essential to restoring confidence. Assist them in their recovery, pay attention to their problems, and allay their fears. Respecting the opinions of stakeholders—whether they be employees, clients, or investors—creates relationships that are more inclusive and trustworthy.

Regular and Reliable Conduct: Conduct that is predictable and regular is necessary to reestablish confidence. Keep your end of the bargain from the crisis recovery phase. Building a commitment to ethical business practices, providing excellent services, and honoring commitments all contribute to restoring trust in the company.

Reparation and Compensation: In situations when stakeholders have suffered losses, providing compensation or reparations may be a concrete step toward restoring confidence. This might be making service improvements, returning money, or taking other actions to address the crises' particular effects on the persons involved.

Learning from errors: Acknowledge the mistakes you made throughout the crisis and share the lessons you learned. Confidence is increased by demonstrating a commitment to ongoing improvement and growth based on those findings. Organizations that are able to grow from their mistakes and adapt are rewarded by stakeholders.

Strategies for Business Recovery

The Strategic Planning Process: Make a thorough recovery strategy that includes important business recovery strategies. This strategy should take long-term sustainability, operational enhancements, and financial stability into account. Strategic planning provides a road map for the rehabilitation process.

Financial Restructuring: Assess and modify the business's financial structure as required. This may include renegotiating contracts, obtaining more funding, or initiating cost-cutting initiatives. A strong financial base is essential to a full recovery.

Operational Optimization: Simplify and increase the efficiency of operational procedures. Identify and address the inefficiencies that came to light during the crisis. An organization model that is more resilient may be achieved via focusing on operational excellence, enhancing supply chain resilience, and using technology.

Adaptability and Innovation: Adopt these two concepts as the fundamental pillars of rehabilitation. Investigate potential new products, services, or markets. Businesses with more capacity for adaptability and change will have a better chance of long-term success.

Employee Engagement and Well-Being: Give attention to the welfare and engagement of your workforce. An inspired and well-supported staff is essential to the healing process. Open communication, measures to boost morale, and training programs result in a strong and focused workforce.

First-Client Approach: Give a customer-focused strategy a lot of consideration. Acknowledge the objectives and needs of your customers, seek their feedback, and modify your offerings accordingly. Regaining the confidence of customers requires constant value delivery and surpassing expectations.

Rebranding and Marketing: Think of rebranding initiatives as a sign of a new beginning. Develop a compelling marketing plan that emphasizes the advancements made in the wake of the tragedy. It is possible to effectively communicate a business' commitment to expansion in order to draw in clients and repair a damaged reputation.

Readiness for a crisis: Using the knowledge gained, create a proactive crisis preparedness strategy. Examine any obstacles and put safety precautions in place. A well-prepared company is better able to deal with unforeseen events in the future and prevent crises from becoming worse.

Restoration and recovery after a corporate catastrophe are difficult tasks requiring a multifaceted strategy. Putting successful recovery processes into place while focusing on rebuilding trust and reputation creates a synergistic path for organizational regeneration.

Effective rehabilitation requires not only overcoming current obstacles but also building a strong basis for the future. By taking this path with integrity, strategic thinking, and a commitment to continuous development, businesses may not only win back stakeholder trust but also come out of it stronger and more resilient than before. In the dynamic commercial market, an organization's capacity to recover and rebuild is a testament to its agility, leadership, and commitment to long-term success.

Conclusion

Essentially, crisis management techniques must adapt constantly to meet the demands of the commercial sector. Instability characterizes the corporate environment, with crises ranging from global pandemics to recessions. The capacity to effectively handle these problems has become essential to an organization's existence and development.

It is not a luxury, but a strategic need to keep improving crisis management. Studying past business crises makes it clear that each one has particular characteristics and necessitates a different course of action. In addition to the uncertainty of the future, prior solutions may not be sufficient to address current challenges. Because the corporate environment is dynamic, crisis management frameworks need to be improved and changed over time.

Analyzing and proactively recognizing potential dangers is an essential part of this progress. Instead than waiting for a catastrophe to strike, organizations are increasingly using preventive measures. This includes creating reaction plans, detecting hazards, and planning scenarios. When businesses are aware of their vulnerabilities and have prepared for a wide range of likely disasters, they are better positioned to react quickly and efficiently when the unexpected happens.

In addition, there has been a significant shift in the field of crisis management since the advancement of technology. Artificial intelligence, advanced analytics, and real-time monitoring systems provide unprecedented capabilities for early detection and quick reaction. Businesses may get useful insights by using these digital innovations, which will enable them to make wise judgments in emergency situations. Adopting these digital technologies requires more than just an increase in output; it also necessitates a fundamental shift in how businesses can proactively manage and reduce risks.

Communication is another important element that highlights how crisis management has evolved. In an era when information is shared instantly, open and prompt communication is essential. Stakeholders, including employees, clients, and the general public, anticipate accurate and fast information during a crisis. Businesses must prioritize sincere and honest communication if they want to maintain their reputation and overcome obstacles.

Maintaining an ongoing emphasis on organizational learning is also necessary for the development of crisis management. After a disaster, evaluations and debriefings provide a priceless chance to gauge how well response plans worked. Not only should areas for improvement be identified and addressed, but also the positive aspects should be emphasized. This iterative learning approach improves preparedness for disasters while also making the company more resilient and flexible overall.

In essence, the corporate world is a dynamic, ever-evolving terrain where crises are inevitable events rather than anomalies. Rather from being a luxury, crisis management's continued expansion is a strategic need. Companies that put a high priority on communication, embrace agility, use technology, and dedicate themselves to learning from every setback will be in a better position to meet the challenges presented by today's fast-paced business climate. In this ongoing process of distinguishing those who thrive in the face of adversity from those who only survive, the ability to enhance crisis management techniques becomes crucial.